ST. ANTONY
OF THE DESERT

"Jesus said to him: No man putting his hand to the plough, and looking back, is fit for the kingdom of God."
—Luke 9:62

St. Athanasius (c. 297-373 A.D.), author of *St. Antony of the Desert,* surrounded by members of his flock as he goes off into exile. Bishop of Alexandria and "The Father of Orthodoxy" against the Arian heresy, St. Athanasius was forced into exile five separate times by various Emperors for upholding the Catholic teaching that Christ is God.

ST. ANTONY
OF THE DESERT

By
St. Athanasius
BISHOP, CONFESSOR AND DOCTOR OF THE CHURCH

Translated from Migne's Greek Text by
Dom J. B. McLaughlin, O.S.B.

"Jesus saith to him: If thou wilt be perfect, go sell what thou hast, and give to the poor, and thou shalt have treasure in heaven: and come follow me."
—Matthew 19:21

TAN BOOKS AND PUBLISHERS, INC.
Rockford, Illinois 61105

Nihil Obstat: F. Thomas Bergh, O.S.B.
                 Censor Deputatus

Imprimatur: Edm. Can. Surmont
                 Vicar General
                 Westminster
                 January 28, 1924

This edition was retypeset from the edition published as *St. Antony the Hermit* by Benziger Brothers, New York, in 1924. (This classic is also known as *The Life of St. Anthony*.)

The type in this book is the property of TAN Books and Publishers, Inc., and may not be reproduced, in whole or in part, without written permission from the Publisher. (This restriction applies to this *type*, not to quotations from the book.)

ISBN: 0-89555-525-5

Library of Congress Catalog Card No.: 95-60545

Cover illustration: St. Antony, Abbot, by Master of the Observance, Musée du Louvre, Paris, © Photo R.M.N.

Printed and bound in the United States of America.

TAN BOOKS AND PUBLISHERS, INC.
P.O. Box 424
Rockford, Illinois 61105

1995

PROMISE OF THE LORD
TO ST. ANTONY OF THE DESERT
After St. Antony Had Withstood
The Snares of the Devil

"Since thou hast endured and not yielded, I will always be thy Helper, and I will make thee renowned everywhere."

(Page 15)

INTRODUCTION

From St. Augustine's Confessions, *Bk. 8, Ch. 6.*

When, therefore, I had declared to him [Pontitianus, a fellow Christian] that I bestowed myself much in the reading of those Scriptures, he took occasion in the course of his speech to discourse unto us of Antony, the Egyptian monk, whose name was excellently famous amongst Thy servants; but, as for us, we had never heard of him until that hour.

But he, so soon as he perceived this, insisted the longer in speaking of him, insinuating the knowledge of so great a man to us, who were wholly ignorant, and wondering withal at that same ignorance of ours. We, on the other hand, were amazed to hear that so lately, and almost in our own days, such wonderful things had been wrought by Thee, in the True Faith and the Catholic Church; so that all of us wondered, we at the hearing of things so strange, and he that we had never heard of them before.

From this he went on to speak of the teeming monasteries, and of them who are a sweet savor unto Thee, and of the fruitful bosom of the barren desert, whereof also we had heard nothing. Nay, more, there was a monastery at Milan, full of holy brethren, close without the walls of the city, under the fostering care of Ambrose, and yet we knew nothing of it. So did he proceed in his discourse, and we held our peace, listening intently. Whereupon he went on to tell us further how once at Trèves, he himself, with three companions, while the Emperor was detained at the afternoon games in the circus, went out to walk in some gardens near the city walls; thus it chanced that they became separated into two parties, one of the three keeping with him and the other two walking together. These latter two, as they wandered up and down, came at length upon a poor cottage, inhabited by divers servants of Thine, *poor in spirit, of whom is the Kingdom of Heaven,* and there they found a book wherein was written the life of Antony.

One of them began to read the same, to wonder at it and to be inflamed by it, and even whilst he was reading to resolve upon leading such a life as that, leaving the service of the world, to become wholly Thine.

ST. ATHANASIUS' PREFACE

It is a good rivalry that you have entered on with the monks in Egypt, trying to equal them or surpass them in your practice of virtue. For with you also there are now monasteries, and the name of monk is in repute. This purpose deserves praise, and may God fulfill it according to your prayers.

And since, too, you have inquired of me about the blessed Antony's way of life, wishing to learn how he began his religious life and what he was before it, and what the end of his life was like and whether the things that are said about him are true, in order to bring yourselves to imitate him; with the greatest willingness I do your bidding. For I, too, gain much help from merely remembering Antony; and I know that you also when you hear, besides admiring the man, will wish to imitate his purpose. For the life of Antony is to monks a sufficient guide to religious life. Do not, then, disbelieve what you have heard about him from those who have told you; rather believe that you have heard but little from them. For indeed it would be very hard for them to relate all, seeing that even I, whatever I may write by letter at your urging, shall yet give you but little account of him. Do you therefore cease not to question those who sail your way, and then perhaps as each tells what he knows, the story may become somewhat more worthy of the man.

Now when I received your letter, I wanted to send for some of the monks who used to be most constantly with him, so that I might learn more and send you a fuller account. But as the sailing season was ending and the letter carrier pressed me, I have hastened to write to your goodness what I myself know (for I saw him often), and what I was able to learn from himself; for I was his assistant for no little time and poured water on his hands. Throughout I have been most careful to give the facts, so that no one need doubt when he hears more; and, on the other hand, that no one may think little of the man through not learning enough about him.

CONTENTS

Book III
ANTONY'S WORK FOR OTHERS

Book IV
ANTONY'S LAST YEARS

ST. ANTONY OF THE DESERT

"And seek not you what you shall eat, or what you shall drink: and be not lifted up on high. For all these things do the nations of the world seek. But your Father knoweth that you have need of these things. But seek ye first the kingdom of God and his justice, and all these things shall be added unto you." —Luke 12:29-31

—Book I—

HOW ANTONY TRAINED HIMSELF

Chapter 1

THE CALL OF GOD

Antony was of Egyptian race, his parents of good birth and good means—Christians too, so that he also was brought up in Christian wise. As a child he lived with his parents, knowing nothing but them and his home; and when he grew to be a boy and was advancing in age, he refused to learn letters, desiring to be away from the company of children. All his wish was, as is written of Jacob, to dwell unspoiled at home. (Cf. *Gen.* 25:27).

With his parents he frequented the church, not with a child's inattention, nor with the contempt of later years, but obeying his parents and listening to the lessons that were read and carefully keeping the fruits of them in his own life. Nor again, though he found himself in a fairly rich home, did he worry his parents for rich and varied food nor care for the enjoyment of it; he was satisfied with what was there and asked no more.

After his parents' death he was left alone with one very young sister. He was eighteen or twenty years old and had charge of the home and of his sister. Less than six months after the death of his

3

parents he was going out to church as usual, and collecting his thoughts, he pondered as he went how the Apostles, leaving all things, followed the Saviour; and the people in the *Acts* who sold their possessions and brought the price and laid it at the feet of the Apostles for distribution among the needy—what good and great hope was laid up in Heaven for these. With these thoughts in his mind, he entered the church; and it so fell that the Gospel was being read then, and he heard the Lord saying to the rich man, *If thou wilt be perfect, go sell all that thou hast and give to the poor, and come follow me and thou shalt have treasure in heaven.* (Cf. *Matt.* 19:21). Then, as though it was from God that his thoughts of the Saints had come and this reading had been for his sake, as soon as he went out of the church he gave to the villagers the property he had from his parents (it was 300 acres of land, fertile and very beautiful) that they might not interfere with him and his sister. And all else that they had in personal property he sold, and raised a fair sum of money, which he gave to the poor, keeping a little because of his sister.

But when, again entering the church, he heard the Lord saying in the Gospel, *Be not solicitous for the morrow* (cf. *Matt.* 6:34), he could not bear to wait longer, but went out and distributed this also to the poor. His sister he commended to known and trusty virgins, and put her with a Sisterhood to be brought up; and then he gave himself for the future to the religious life, minding himself and living a life of hardship, in front of his own house. For as yet monasteries were not so universal in Egypt, and no monk yet knew the great desert; but each who wished to attend to his soul exercised himself alone not far from his own village.

Now there was at the time in the neighboring village an old man who had practiced the solitary life from youth. Antony, seeing him, was eager to imitate him, so he too at first began to stay in the places near the village. From there, if he heard anywhere of an earnest soul, he went forth like a wise bee and sought him out; nor would he return to his own place till he had seen him and got from him what would help him on his way to virtue; then he went back. There, then, he made his first steps, steadying his mind not to turn back to his inheritance nor to think of his kindred, but to give all its desire and all its energy to keeping up the religious life. He worked with his hands, having heard, *if any man will not work, neither let him eat* (cf. *2 Thess.* 3:10), spending the money partly on bread, partly on the poor. He prayed constantly, having learned that in private we must pray without ceasing. (Cf. *Luke* 18:1). For he so listened to the reading that nothing of what is written escaped him, but he retained everything, and for the future his memory served him instead of books.

Living this manner of life, Antony was beloved

by all. He made himself really subject to the devout men whom he visited and learned for himself the special religious virtues of each of them: the graciousness of one, the continual prayer of another; he observed the meekness of one, the charity of another; studied one in his long watchings, another in his love of reading; admired one for his steadfastness, another for his fasting and sleeping on the ground; watched one's mildness, another's patience; while in all alike he remarked the same reverence for Christ and the same love for each other. Having thus gathered his fill, he returned to his own place of discipline and thereafter pondered with himself what he had learned from each and strove to show in himself the virtues of all. He had no contentions with those of his own age, save only that he would not be found second to them in the better things; and this he did in such manner that none was grieved, but they too were glad on his account. Seeing him such, then, all the village people and the devout with whom he had intercourse called him a man of God and loved him as a son or as a brother.

Chapter 2

FIRST TEMPTATIONS

But the devil, the hater and envier of good, could not bear to see such resolution in a young man, but attempted to use against him the means in which he is skilled. First he tried to draw him back from the religious life by reminding him of his property, of the care of his sister, his intimacy with his kindred, the love of money, the love of fame, the manifold pleasures of the table and the other relaxations of life—and lastly the hardness of virtue and how great is the labor thereof, suggesting that the body is weak and time is long. So he raised in his mind a great dust cloud of arguments to drive him aside from his straight purpose. But when the enemy saw himself powerless in face of Antony's resolution and that rather he was himself overthrown by his firmness and routed by his much faith and beaten by Antony's constant prayer, then placing his trust in "the weapons that hang at his waist" (cf. *Job* 40:11) and glorying in these (for these are his first snare against the young), he advanced against the young man, disturbing him by night and so besetting him by day that even onlookers could see the struggle that was going on between the two. He suggested evil thoughts, and the other turned them away by his prayers. He roused feelings, and Antony, ashamed, defended himself by faith and prayers and fastings. The wretched fiend even stooped to masquerade as a woman by night, simply to deceive Antony; and he quenched the fire of that temptation by thinking of Christ and of the nobility we have through Him, and of the dignity of the soul. (Cf. *1 Cor.* 6:15). Again the enemy suggested the delight of pleasure; but he, angered and grieved, thought over the threat of the fire and the torment of the worm. (Cf. *Mark* 9:43). These he opposed to his temptations and so came through them unhurt. So all these things turned to the confusion of the adversary, for he who thought to be like to God was now mocked by a youth, and he who gloried over flesh and blood was now defeated by a man clad in the flesh. For with him wrought the Lord, who for us took flesh and gave to the body the victory over the devil, so that those who truly strive can each say, *"Not I, but the grace of God with me."* (*1 Cor.* 15:10).

As neither by this means could the serpent conquer Antony, but saw himself thrust out of his heart, at length, gnashing his teeth as it is written (cf. *Ps.* 111:10), like one in a frenzy, he showed himself in appearance as he is in mind, coming to Antony in the shape of a black boy and as it were flattering him. He no longer assailed him with thoughts, for the deceiver had been cast out, but using now a human voice, he said, "Many have I deceived, and very many have I overthrown; yet now, when I attacked you and your works as I have attacked others, I was not strong enough." Antony asked, "Who are you that say such things to me?" Then at once he answered in piteous tones, "I am the lover of uncleanness; I take charge of the ensnaring and the tempting of the young; and I am called the spirit of fornication. How many have I deceived who meant to be careful! How many that were chaste have I drawn away with temptations. I am he through whom the prophet reproaches the fallen, saying: You were deceived by a spirit of fornication, for it was through me that they were tripped up. I am he that so often beset you and as often was defeated by you." Then Antony thanked God, and taking courage against him, said to him, "Then you are much to be despised, for your mind is black and your strength as a child's. I have not one anxiety left on your account, for *'the Lord is my helper, and I will despise my enemies.'*" (Cf. *Ps.* 117:7). Hearing this, the black spirit instantly fled, cowering at his words and fearing even to approach the man.

This was Antony's first victory over the devil; or rather, this was the triumph in Antony of the Saviour, *who condemned sin in the flesh, that the justice of the law may be fulfilled in us, who walk not according to the flesh, but according to the spirit.* (Cf. *Rom.* 8:3, 4).

But thereafter Antony did not grow careless and neglect himself, as though the devil were beaten; neither did the enemy cease his wiles, as having failed. For he wandered round again like a lion seeking some chance against him. And Antony, having learned from the Scriptures that the craftinesses of the enemy are many (cf. *Luke* 10:19), gave himself earnestly to the religious life, deeming that, though the foe had not been able to beguile his heart with bodily pleasures, he would surely try to ensnare him by other means—for the devil is a lover of sin. More and more, therefore, did he repress the body and bring it into subjection, lest after winning at one point, he should be dragged down at another. He decided, therefore, to accustom himself to harder ways. And many wondered, but he easily bore the hardship, for the eagerness of the spirit, long abiding with him, wrought in him a good habit; so that a small occasion given by others led him to a great exercise of zeal. For such was his watching that often he passed the whole night unsleeping; and this not once, but it was seen with wonder that he did it most frequently. He ate once in the day, after sunset, and at times he broke his fast only after two days—and often even after four days. His food was bread and salt, his drink only water. Of meat and wine it is needless to speak, for nothing of this sort was to be found among the other monks either. For sleep a rush mat sufficed him; as a rule he simply lay on the ground. The oiling of the skin he refused, saying that it were better for young men to prefer exercise and not seek for things that make the body soft—rather to accustom it to hardships, mindful of the Apostle's words: *When I am weak, then am I strong.* (Cf. *2 Cor.* 12:10). For he said that when the enjoyments of the body are weak, then is the power of the soul strong.

He had also this strange-seeming principle: he held that not by length of time is the way of virtue measured and our progress therein, but by desire and by strong resolve. Accordingly, he himself gave no thought to the bygone time, but each day, as though then beginning his religious life, he made greater effort to advance, constantly repeating to himself St. Paul's saying: *Forgetting the things that are behind, and reaching out to the things that are before* (cf. *Phil.* 3:13); keeping in mind, too, the voice of Elias the Prophet saying, *The Lord liveth, before whose sight I stand this day.* (Cf. *3 Kings* 17:1). For he observed that in saying *this day,* he did not count the bygone time; but as though always making a beginning, he was earnest each day to present himself such as one ought to appear before God: clean of heart and ready to obey His will and none other. And he used to say within himself that from the way of life of the great Elias a religious man must always study his own way of life, as in a mirror.

Chapter 3

HIS LIFE IN THE TOMBS

Having thus mastered himself, Antony departed to the tombs that lay far from the village, having asked one of his acquaintance to bring him bread from time to time. He entered one of the tombs, his friend closed the door of it on him, and he remained alone within. This the enemy would not endure, for he feared lest by degrees Antony should fill the desert too with monks. Coming one night with a throng of demons, he so scourged him that he lay on the ground speechless from the pain. For, he declared, the pain was so severe that blows from men could not have caused such agony. By God's providence (for the Lord does not overlook those who hope in Him), his friend came the next day bringing him bread, and when he opened the door and saw him lying on the ground, as dead, he lifted him and took him to the village church and laid him on the ground. Many of his kin and the village people watched beside Antony as for one dead. But towards midnight Antony came to himself and awoke, and seeing all asleep and only his friend waking, he signed to him to come near and asked him to lift him again and carry him back to the tombs without waking anyone.

So he was carried back by the man, and the door was closed as before, and he was again alone within. He could not stand because of the blows, but he prayed lying down. And after his prayer, he shouted out, "Here am I, Antony; I do not run away from your blows. For though you should give me yet more, nothing shall separate me from the love of Christ." (Cf. *Rom.* 8:35). Then he sang the Psalm, *If armies in camp should stand together against me, my heart shall not fear.* (Cf. *Ps.* 26:3).

The monk, then, thought and spoke thus. But the enemy of all good, marveling that even after the blows he had courage to go back, called together his hounds and burst out in fury, "Do you see that we have not stopped this man, either by the spirit of fornication or by blows, but he challenges us; let us attack him another way." For plans of ill are easy to the devil.

Thereupon in the night they made such a crashing that it seemed the whole place was shaken by an earthquake; and as if they had broken through the four walls of the building, the demons seemed to rush in through them in the guise of beasts and creeping things, and the place was at once filled with the forms of lions, bears, leopards, bulls, serpents, asps, scorpions and wolves. And each moved according to its own likeness. The lion roared, ready to spring, the bull seemed thrusting with its horns, the serpent crept yet reached him not, the wolf held itself as if ready to strike. And the noise of all the visions was terrible, and their fury cruel.

Antony, beaten and goaded by them, felt keener bodily pain. Nevertheless he lay fearless and more alert in spirit. He groaned with the soreness of his body, but in mind he was cool and said jestingly, "If you had any power in you, it would have been enough that just one of you should come; but the Lord has taken your strength away, and that is why you try to frighten me, if possible, by your numbers. It is a sign of your helplessness that you have taken the shapes of brutes." Again he said cheerily, "If you can, and if you have received power over me, do not wait, but lay on. But if you cannot, why are you chafing yourselves for nothing? For our trust in the Lord is like a seal to us, and like a wall of safety."

So, after making many attempts, they gnashed their teeth at him because they were befooling themselves and not him.

And the Lord in this also forgot not Antony's wrestling, but came to his defense. For looking up, Antony saw as it were the roof opening and a beam of light coming down to him. And the demons suddenly disappeared, and the soreness of his body ceased at once, and the building was again sound.

Antony, seeing that help was come, breathed more freely, being eased of his pains. And he asked the vision, "Where wert Thou? Why didst

Thou not show Thyself from the beginning, to end my suffering?" And a voice came to him: "I was here, Antony, but I waited to see thy resistance. Therefore since thou hast endured and not yielded, I will always be thy Helper, and I will make thee renowned everywhere." Hearing this Antony arose and prayed, and he was so strengthened that he perceived that he had more power in his body than formerly. He was at this time about thirty-five years old.

Chapter 4

ALONE IN THE DESERT
(At Pispir, now Der el Memun)

The next day, going out with still greater zeal for the service of God, Antony met the old man before mentioned and asked him to live in the desert with him. He refused because of his age and because this was not as yet usual, but Antony at once set out for the mountain. Yet once more the enemy, seeing his zeal and wishing to check it, threw in his way the form of a large disc of silver. Antony, understanding the deceit of the Evil One, stood and looked at the disc and confuted the demon in it, saying, "Whence a disc in the desert? This is not a trodden road, and there is no track of any faring this way. And it could not have fallen unnoticed, being of huge size. And even if it had been lost, the loser would certainly have found it had he turned back to look, because the place is desert. This is a trick of the devil. You will not hinder my purpose by this, Satan; let this thing perish with thee." And as Antony said this, it disappeared like smoke before the face of the fire.

Now as he went on, he again saw, not this time a phantom, but real gold lying in the way.

Whether it was the enemy that pointed it out or whether it was a higher power, training the disciple and proving to the devil that he cared nothing even for real riches, he himself did not say, and we do not know—only that it was gold that he saw. Antony marveled at the quantity, but avoided it like fire and passed on without looking back, running swiftly on till he lost sight of the place and knew not where it was.

So with firmer and firmer resolution, he went to the mountain, and finding beyond the river a fort, long deserted and now full of reptiles, he betook himself there and dwelt in it. The reptiles fled at once as though chased by someone; and he, closing up the entrance and laying in bread for six months (the Thebans do this, and often it keeps unspoiled for a whole year), and having water in the fort, went down into the inner rooms and abode there alone, not going out himself and not seeing any who came to visit him. For a long time he continued this life of asceticism, only receiving his loaves twice in the year from the house above.

His acquaintances who came to see him often spent days and nights outside, since he would not let them enter. They seemed to hear a tumultuous crowd inside, making noises, uttering piteous cries, shrieking, "Stand off from our domain! What have you to do with the desert? You cannot stand against our contrivings." At first those outside thought there were men fighting with Antony, who had got in to him by a ladder, but when they

bent down through a hole and saw no one, then
they thought it was demons and feared for themselves and called to Antony. He listened to them,
though he gave no thought to the demons; and
going near to the door, he urged the people to
go home and fear not, saying that the demons
made these displays against the timid. "Do you
therefore sign yourselves and go away bravely and
leave them to make fools of themselves." So they
went away, protecting themselves with the Sign of
the Cross, and he remained and was nowise hurt
by them. Nor did he weary of the struggle. For
the aid of the visions that came to him from on
high and the weakness of his enemies brought him
much ease from his labors and prepared him for
greater earnestness. His friends used to come constantly, expecting to find him dead; but they heard
him singing: *Let God arise, and let his enemies
be scattered: and let them that hate him flee from
before his face. As smoke vanisheth, so let them
vanish away: as wax melteth before the fire, so
let the wicked perish at the presence of God.* (Ps.
67:2-3). And again: *All the nations surrounded
me, and by the name of the Lord I drove them
off.* (Cf. Ps. 117:10).

He spent nearly twenty years in this solitary religious life, neither going out nor being seen regu-
larly by any. After that, many longed and sought
to copy his holy life, and some of his friends came
and forcibly broke down the door and removed
it; and Antony came forth as from a holy of

holies, filled with heavenly secrets and possessed by the Spirit of God. This was the first time he showed himself from the fort to those who came to him. When they saw him they marveled to see that his body kept its former state, being neither grown heavy for want of exercise, nor shrunken with fastings and strivings against demons. For he was such as they had known him before his retirement. The light of his soul, too, was absolutely pure. It was not shrunk with grieving nor dissipated by pleasure; it had no touch of levity nor of gloom. He was not bashful at seeing the crowd nor elated at being welcomed by such numbers, but was unvaryingly tranquil, a man ruled by reason, whose whole character had grown firm-set in the way that nature had meant it to grow.

Through him the Lord healed many of those present who were suffering from bodily ills and freed others from evil spirits. And the Lord gave Antony grace in speech, so that he comforted many in sorrow; others who were at strife he made friends; charging all not to prefer anything in the world to the love of Christ. And when he spoke and exhorted them to be mindful of the good things to come and of the love of God for us, who *spared not his own Son, but delivered him up for us all* (cf. *Rom.* 8:32), he induced many to take up the solitary life. And so from that time there were monasteries in the mountains, and the desert was peopled with monks who went forth from their own and became citizens of the kingdom of Heaven.

—Book II—

ANTONY'S TEACHINGS

Chapter 5

WHAT A MONK'S VOCATION IS

When he had need to cross the canal of Arsenoe (the need was his visitation of the brethren), the canal was full of crocodiles. And simply praying, he entered it with all his companions, and they passed through unhurt.

He returned to the monastery and continued the same holy and generous labors. He preached constantly, increasing the zeal of those who were already monks and stirring many others to the love of the religious life; and soon, as the word drew men, the number of monasteries became very great; and to all he was a guide and a father.

One day, when he had gone out and all the monks came to him asking to hear a discourse, he spoke to them as follows in the Egyptian tongue:

The Scriptures are enough for our instruction. Yet it is well that we should encourage each other in the Faith and stimulate each other with words. Do you, therefore, bring what you know and tell it like children to your father; while I, as your elder, share with you what I know and have experienced. First of all, let one same zeal be common to all, not to give up what we have begun, not to be faint-hearted in our labors, not to say we have lived long in this service, but rather as beginners to have greater zeal each day. For the whole life of a man is very short, measured beside the ages to come, so that all our time is nothing compared to eternal life. And in the world, every merchandise is sold at its worth, and men barter like value for like. But the promise of eternal life is bought for a trifle. For it is written: *The days of our years. . .are threescore and ten years. But if in the strong they be fourscore years: and what is more of them is labour and sorrow.* (Cf. *Ps.* 89:10). If, then, we spend the whole eighty years in the religious life, or even a hundred, we shall not reign for the like space of a hundred years, but in return for the hundred, we shall reign through ages of ages. And if our striving is on earth, our inheritance shall not be on earth, but in Heaven is our promised reward. Our body, too, we give up corruptible; we receive it back incorruptible.

Therefore, children, let us not faint, nor weary, nor think we are doing much: *For the sufferings of this present time are not worthy to be compared to the glory that shall be revealed to us.* (Cf. *Rom.* 8:18). Neither let us look back to the world, thinking that we have renounced much. For the whole earth is but a narrow thing compared to all Heaven. If, then, we were lords of the whole earth, and renounced the whole earth, that, too, would be worth nothing beside the kingdom of Heaven. As though a man should make light of one bronze coin to gain a hundred pieces of gold, so he that owns all the earth, and renounces it, gives up but little and receives a hundredfold. If, then, the whole earth is no price for Heaven, surely he who has given up a few acres must not boast nor grow careless, for what he forsakes is as nothing, even if he leave a home and much wealth.

There is another thing to consider: if we do not forsake these things for virtue's sake, still we leave them later on when we die—and often, as *Ecclesiastes* reminds us, to those whom we would not. (Cf. *Eccles.* 2:18). Then why not leave them for virtue's sake and to inherit a kingdom?

Therefore let none of us have even the wish to possess. For what profit is it to possess these things which yet we cannot take with us? Why not rather possess those things which we can take away with us—prudence, justice, temperance, fortitude, understanding, charity, love of the poor, gentleness, hospitality? For if we gain these possessions, we shall find them going beforehand, to make a welcome for us there in the land of the meek.

With these thoughts let a man urge himself not to grow careless, especially if he considers that he is one of God's servants, and owes service to his master. Now as a servant would not dare to say, "Today I do not work because I worked yesterday," nor would count up the time that is past and rest in the coming days; but each day, as is written in the Gospel (cf. *Luke* 17:7-8), shows the same willingness, in order to keep his Lord's favor and avoid danger; so too let us too daily abide in our service, knowing that if we are slovenly for one day, He will not pardon us for the sake of the bygone time, but will be angry with us for slighting Him. So have we heard in Ezechiel (cf. *Ezech.* 3:20); so, too, Judas in one night destroyed all his toil in the foregone time. (Cf. *John* 6:71- 72).

Therefore, children, let us hold fast the religious life and not grow careless. For in this we have the Lord working with us, as it is written, *God cooperates unto good with everyone that chooseth the good.* (Cf. *Rom.* 8:28). And to prevent negligence, it is well for us to ponder on the Apostle's saying: *I die daily.* (*1 Cor.* 15:31). For if we also so live as dying daily, we shall not sin. What is meant is this: that when we wake each day, we should think we shall not live till evening; and again, when we go to sleep, we should think we shall not wake, for our life is of its nature uncertain and is measured out to us daily by Providence. So thinking and so living from day to day, we shall not sin, nor shall we have any longing for anything, nor cherish wrath against anyone, nor lay up treasure on the earth; but as men who each day expect to die, we shall be poor, we shall forgive everything to all men. The desire of women and of evil pleasure we shall—not meet and master—but we shall turn away from it as a fleeting thing, striving always, and always looking to the Day of Judgment. (Cf. *Luke* 12:5). For the greater fear and the danger of torment always break the delight of pleasure and steady the wavering mind.

Having made a beginning and set out on the way of virtue, let us stretch out yet more to reach the things that are before us. Let none turn back like Lot's wife, especially as the Lord has said: *No man setting his hand to the plough and turning back is fit for the kingdom of heaven. (Luke* 9:62). Turning back simply means changing one's mind and caring again for worldly things.

And when you hear of virtue, do not fear nor feel the word strange; for it is not afar from us, not something that stands without; no, the thing is within us, and the doing it easy, if only we have the will. The Greeks go abroad and cross the sea to study letters, but we have no need to go abroad for the kingdom of Heaven, nor to cross the sea after virtue. For the Lord has told us beforehand: *The kingdom of heaven is within you. (Luke* 17:21). Virtue, therefore, needs only our will, since it is within us and grows from us. For virtue grows when the soul keeps the understanding according to nature. It is according to nature when it remains as it was made. Now it was made beautiful and perfectly straight. For this reason Josue, the son of Nave, commanded the people: *Make straight your hearts to your ways. (Cf. Josue*

24:23). For the straightness of the soul consists in the mind's being according to nature, as it was made; as, on the other hand, the soul is said to be evil when it bends and gets twisted away from what is according to nature. So the task is not difficult: if we remain as God made us, we are in virtue; if we give our minds to evil, we are accounted wicked. If, then, it were a thing that must be sought from without, the task would indeed be hard; but if it be within us, let us guard ourselves from evil thoughts and keep our soul for the Lord, as a trust we have received from Him, that He may recognize His work, finding it as it was when He made it.

Let us fight also not to be mastered by anger nor enslaved by concupiscence. For it is written that *the anger of man worketh not the justice of God.* (*James* 1:20). And *concupiscence, having conceived, bringeth forth sin; and sin, when it is completed, bringeth forth death.* (Cf. *James* 1:15).

Chapter 6

OF THE ASSAULTS OF DEMONS

Living this life, let us watch ceaselessly, and as it is written, guard our heart with all watchfulness. (Cf. *Prov.* 4:23). For we have enemies, terrible and unscrupulous, the wicked demons, and against them is our warfare, as the Apostle said, *not against flesh and blood, but against principalities and powers, against the rulers of the world of this darkness, against the spirits of wickedness dwelling in the high places.* (*Eph.* 6:12). Great is the number of them in the air around us, and they are not far from us. But there is much difference in them. It would be long to speak of their nature and differences, and such a discourse is for others greater than us; the only pressing and necessary thing now is to know their treacheries against us.

Let us first understand this, that the demons were not made as demons, for God made nothing bad. But they also were created beautiful, but fell from heavenly wisdom; and thenceforward, wandering about the earth, they have deceived the Greeks with their apparitions. They envy us Christians and move everything to hinder us from the way to Heaven, lest we mount to where they fell from. Therefore there is needed much prayer and self-discipline, that a man may receive from the Holy Ghost the gift of discerning spirits and may be able to know about them—which of them are less wicked, and which more, and in what kind of thing each of them is interested, and how each is defeated and cast out. For they have many treacheries and many moves in their plotting. The blessed Apostle and his followers knew this, saying: *We are not ignorant of his contrivings.* (2 Cor. 2:11). And we, from being tempted by them, must guide one another. Therefore, as having in part experience of them, I speak to you as my children.

If, then, they see any Christians, but especially monks, laboring gladly and making progress, they first attack them and tempt them by putting continual stumbling blocks in their way. These stumbling blocks are bad thoughts. We must not fear their suggestions, for by prayers and fastings and trust in the Lord they are defeated at once. Yet when defeated they do not cease, but come back again wickedly and deceitfully. For when they cannot mislead the heart with plainly unclean delights, they attack again in another way and try to frighten it by weaving phantoms, taking the forms of women, of beasts and reptiles, and gigantic bodies, and armies of soldiers. But even so, we must not fear their phantoms, for they are nothing and quickly disappear, especially if one fortify himself with faith and the Sign of the Cross. But they are daring and utterly shameless.

For if here too they are beaten, they come on again in another way. They pretend to prophesy and to foretell things to come, and to show themselves taller than the roof and as vast phantoms to those whom they could not beguile with thoughts. And if even so they find the soul firm in faith and in the hope of its purpose, then they bring in their leader.

Often, he said, they appear in shape such as the Lord revealed the devil to Job, saying: *His eyes are like the look of the dawn. From his mouth come forth burning lamps, and fires are shot forth. From his nostrils comes the smoke of a furnace, burning with a fire of coals. His breath is coals, and flame proceeds from his mouth.* (Cf. *Job* 41:9-12). When the leader of the devils appears in this way, the wretch causes terror, as I said, boasting as the Lord described, saying to Job: *He esteemed iron as chaff, and bronze as rotten wood; he thought the sea a vessel for ointments, the deeps of hell a captive; he judged the deeps to be a place for walking* (cf. *Job* 41:18); and by the mouth of the Prophet: *The enemy said, I will pursue and will capture* (cf. *Ex.* 15:9); and by another: *I will grasp the whole world in my hand like a nest, and as deserted eggs will I seize it.* (Cf. *Isaias* 10:14). And all such boastings and threatenings they make, seeking to deceive the devout. Here, again, we faithful must not fear his appearances nor heed his words. For he lies, and there is no truth at all in his speech. For he talks thus and makes so bold, ignoring how he was dragged away with a hook like a serpent by the Saviour, was haltered like a beast of burden, was ringed through the nostrils like a runaway, and his lips pierced with an armlet. (Cf. *Job* 40:19). The Lord has tethered him as a sparrow, to be mocked at by us. (Cf. *Job* 40:24). He and his demons are put like scorpions and snakes to be trodden under foot by us Christians. A proof of this is our now living this life in spite of him. For he that threatened to wipe up the sea and to grasp the world, now, behold, cannot hinder our devotion, cannot even stop me speaking against him. Therefore, let us not heed whatever he may say, for he lies, nor fear his lying visions. For it is no true light that is seen in them; rather, they bring a foretaste and likeness of the fire that was prepared for them. They seek to frighten men with that in which themselves shall burn. They appear, but at once they disappear again, having hurt no one, and taking with them the likeness of the fire that is to receive them. So we need not fear them on this account either, for by the grace of Christ all their practicings are to no purpose. They are treacherous and ready to take on them any part and any shape. Often, without appearing, they pretend to sing psalms and repeat sayings from the Scripture. Sometimes, when we are reading, they will repeat at once like an echo the very words we have read. When we are asleep, they wake us to prayers, and this persistently, scarcely letting us get to sleep. At times, too, they take the shape of monks and pretend to talk piously, in order to deceive by the likeness of form, and then lead whither they will those whom they have beguiled. But we must not heed them, though they wake us to pray, though they advise us to fast altogether, though they pretend to accuse and reproach us for things wherein once they were our accomplices. Not for piety nor for truth's sake do they do this, but in order to bring the simple into despair, and to say that asceticism avails not, and to make men disgusted with the monastic life as burdensome and most grievous, and to entangle those whose life is contrary to them.

Against such as these the prophet sent by God pronounces woe, saying: *Woe to him that giveth his neighbour a troubled drink to turn him back.* (Cf. *Hab.* 2:15). For such devices and thoughts turn men back in the way that leads to virtue. And Our Lord Himself, even when the demons spoke the truth (for they truly said, Thou art the Son of God), yet silenced them and forbade them to speak, lest after the truth they should oversow their own wickedness, and also to teach us never to heed them, even though they seem to speak truth, for it is unseemly that we who have the Holy Scriptures—and the freedom of Christ— should be taught by the devil, who kept not his own rank, but is minded now one way, now another. (Cf. *Jude*). Therefore, He forbids him to speak, even to quote the words of Scripture: *To the sinful one God said, Why do you relate my judgements and take my testament into your mouth?* (Cf. *Ps.* 49:16). For they do everything; they talk, they make an uproar, they pretend, they unsettle the mind, all to deceive the simple, making a din, laughing senselessly, hissing. And if one heed them not, they weep and wail as defeated.

The Lord, then, being God, silenced the demons. But we, learning from the Saints, must do as they did and imitate their courage. For they, when they saw these things, said: *When the sinner stood against me, I was dumb, and was humbled, and kept silence from good things.* (Cf. *Ps.* 38:2). And again: *But I, as a deaf man, heard not: and as a dumb man not opening his mouth: and I became as a man that heareth not.* (Cf. *Ps.* 37:14). Wherefore let us not listen to them; they are none of ours. Nor let us hearken, though they call us to prayer or speak of fastings. But rather, let us attend to our own purpose of holy living and not be cheated by them who do all deceitfully. We must not fear them, though they seem to assault us or threaten death, for they are powerless and can do nothing but threaten.

This much I have said of them in passing. But now we must not shrink from a fuller discourse about them; it will be safer for you to be warned.

Chapter 7

THE DEVIL'S POWERLESSNESS

Since Our Lord lived, the enemy is fallen, and his powers have lost their strength. Therefore, though he can do nothing, nevertheless, like a fallen tyrant, he does not rest, but threatens, though it be but words. Let each of you think of that, and he can despise the demons. If they were tied to such bodies as we are, they might then say, "We cannot find men who hide, but if we do find them, we hurt them." And we in that case might escape them by hiding and locking doors against them. But since they are not so, but can enter where doors are locked, and since they are found in all the air, they and their chief, the devil, and since they are evil-willed and ready to hurt— and as Our Lord said: *the father of evil, the devil, is a murderer from the beginning (John 8:44)*— and nevertheless, we live and carry on our life in defiance of them, it is evident that they have no power. Place does not hinder them from plotting; and they do not see us friendly to them, that they should spare us; and they have no love of justice, that they should amend. On the contrary, they are wicked and desire nothing so much as to injure those who seek virtue and honor God. The reason they do nothing is because they can do nothing, except threaten; if they could, they would not wait, but would do the evil at once, since their will is quite ready for it, especially against us. Look: here are we now gathered and talking against them; and they know that, as we advance, they grow weak. If, then, they had power, they would not have let one of us Christians live, for the service of God is an abomination to the sinner. As they can do nothing, they rather injure themselves in this, for they cannot do aught of what they threaten.

Again, this must be remembered, to end all fear of them. If any power belonged to them, they would not come in a crowd, nor cause phantoms, nor use devices and appearances; it would be enough that one alone should come and do what he could and would. Anyone who really has power does not destroy with phantoms nor frighten with crowds, but uses his power at once as he wills. But the demons, who have no power, play as on a stage, changing their forms and frightening children by the look of numbers and by their shapes; for all which they are the more to be despised as powerless. The real angel who was sent by God against the Assyrians needed not crowds, nor visible phantoms, nor clangings, nor clappings, but quietly used his power and destroyed a hundred and eighty-five thousand of them. Whereas helpless demons like these try to frighten, if only by shadows.

Now if anyone thinks of the case of Job and asks, "Why then did the devil go forth and do everything against him—strip him of his possessions, destroy his children and strike him with a grievous ulcer?" let such a one know that it was not the devil who had power, but God who gave Job into his hands to be tried. Because he had no power to do anything, he asked and received, and did it. Herein, therefore, is the more reason to despise the enemy, that though he desired, he was powerless against one just man. Had he had power, he would not have asked for it. He asked, not once, but a second time; plainly he is weak and helpless. And little wonder he was powerless against Job, when he could not destroy even his beasts unless God had permitted. Not even against swine has he power, for as it is written in the Gospel: *They entreated the Lord saying, Suffer us to depart into the swine.* (*Mark* 5:12). If they have no power over swine, much less have they over men made in the likeness of God.

God only must we fear, then; these creatures we must despise and nowise fear. Indeed, the more they do, the more effort must we make on our way in defiance of them. For the great weapon against them is a right life and confidence in God. For they dread the ascetics' fasting, watching, prayers, meekness, peacefulness, their scorn of wealth and of vainglory, their humility, love of the poor, alms-deeds, their mildness, and most of all, their devotion to Christ. This is why they do all they can that there may be none to trample on them: for they know the grace that the Saviour gave to His faithful against them when He said: *Behold I have given you power to trample on serpents and scorpions and on all the strength of the enemy.* (*Luke* 10:19).

Chapter 8

THE DEVIL'S PROPHECIES

Further, if they pretend also to prophesy, let no one heed. For often they tell us days beforehand of brothers who are coming to see us; and they do come. It is not from kindness to their hearers that they do this, but in order to induce these to trust them, and thereafter, having them in their power, to destroy them. Wherefore we must not listen to them, but even as they speak must repulse them; for we have no need of them. For what wonder is it if they whose bodies are of subtler nature than men's, when they have seen some of the brethren beginning a journey, outrun them and announce them? So does a horseman bring word, outstripping those who go on foot. So here, too, we need not marvel at them. They foreknow naught of what has not yet happened; God alone knows all things before they come to birth. But these, like thieves, run ahead and bring word what they have seen. Even at this moment to how many do they make known our doings, how we are assembled and hold discourse against them, before any goes from us to give the news! This, too, a fleet-footed boy might do, outstripping a slower.

What I mean is this: If someone begins to travel from the Thebaid or any other place, they do not know if he will travel till he starts. But when they see him on the way, they run ahead and bring word before he comes; and so it is that after some days the traveler comes. Yet often enough their news is false, for the travelers turn back.

So, too, at times they chatter about the water of the river. Seeing great rains falling in the parts of Ethiopia, and knowing that from there comes the flooding of the river, they run ahead and tell it before the water reaches Egypt. Men could tell it too, if they could run as these. And as David's scout (cf. 2 Kgs. 18:24), mounting a height, saw better who was coming than one who stayed below; and as even he who ran ahead told before the rest not things unborn, but things that had come to pass and were on the way; so these choose to hurry and bring news to others simply to deceive them. But if in the meantime Providence arrange aught concerning the waters or the travelers, as it can, then the demons have spoken falsely and they who heeded them are deceived.

It was thus that the Greek oracles arose and men were formerly deceived by the demons, but it is thus, too, that the deceit is ended henceforward. For the Lord came, who has made void the demons and all their wickedness. For of themselves they know nothing, but they see what knowledge others have, and like thieves take it and twist it. They are guessers rather than prophets.

Therefore, if sometimes they foretell such things truly, even so no one need wonder at them. For physicians also who have experience of diseases, when they meet the same disease in others, can often tell beforehand, judging from experience. And again, seamen and farmers, looking at the state of the weather, from their experience prophesy that there will be a storm or fine weather. No one would say because of this that they prophesy by supernatural inspiration, but by experience and practice. Wherefore, if the demons too sometimes say these same things by conjecture, they are not to be admired or heeded on that account. For what profit is it to the hearers to learn from them days beforehand what is coming; or what manner of eagerness to know such things, even could one know them truly? For this makes not for virtue, neither is it any mark of goodness. For none of us is judged for that [which] he knows not, and none is blessed for that [which] he has learned and knows; but on these things each has to be judged—if he has held fast the Faith, and truly kept the Commandments.

Therefore, we must not make much of these things, nor live our life of hardship and toil for the sake of knowing the future, but in order to please God by living well. And we must pray, not in order to know the future, nor is that the reward we must ask for our hard life, but that Our Lord may be our fellow-worker in conquering the devil. But if ever we care to know the future, let us be pure in mind. For I am sure that, when a soul is pure on all sides and in her natural state, she becomes clear-sighted and can see more and further than the demons, having the Lord to show her, as was the soul of Eliseus when watching the doings of Giezi, and seeing the armies that stood by them. (Cf. *4 Kgs.* 5:26; 6:17).

Chapter 9

HOW TO DISTINGUISH GOOD FROM BAD VISIONS

When they come to you by night and want to tell the future, or say, "We are the angels," do not heed, for they lie. And if they praise your strict life, and call you blessed, do not you hearken nor deal with them at all. Rather, bless yourselves and bless the house, and pray, and you will see them disappear. For they are cowards and utterly dread the sign of our Lord's Cross, since it was on the Cross that the Saviour despoiled them and exposed them. (Cf. *Col.* 2:25). But if they stay unashamed, with dancing and changing shows, do you not fear nor shrink, neither give heed to them as being good spirits. For to distinguish the presence of the good and the bad is by God's gift possible and easy. A vision of holy ones is not troubled, *for he shall not contend, nor cry out, neither shall any man hear his voice* (cf. *Matt.* 12:19); but it falls so restfully and gently that instant gladness and joy and courage awake in the soul. For with the holy visitants is Our Lord, who is our joy and God the Father's might. The soul's thoughts remain untroubled and calm, so that she

looks on her visitants enlightened in herself.
There comes on her a longing for heavenly things
and things to come, and she is ready to be wholly
united to them if she might go with them. And
if some, being human, tremble at the vision of
good angels, then at once the angel dispels the
fear by love, as did Gabriel for Zachary (cf. *Luke*
1:13), and the angel who appeared in the holy
sepulchre for the women (cf. *Mark* 16:6), and
he that said to the shepherds in the Gospel, *Fear
not.* (Cf. *Luke* 2:10). For their fear is not from
cowardice of soul, but from feeling the presence
of higher natures. Such then is the vision of holy
ones.

But the assault and appearance of the evil ones
is troubled, with crashing and din and outcry, as
might be the rioting of rough youths and thieves.
From which comes at once terror of soul, distur-
bance and disorder of thoughts, dejection, hatred
of ascetics, recklessness, sadness, the memory of
one's family, the fear of death; and then a craving
for evil, a contempt of virtue and an unsettling
of the character. When, therefore, you see someone and are afraid, if the fear is immediately taken
from you and instead of it comes joy unspeakable,
cheerfulness, courage and recovery, and calmness
of thought, and the rest that I have named,
strength, and love of God, then be of good cheer,
and pray, for the joy and the steadiness of the soul
show the holiness of the Presence. So Abraham
(cf. *John* 8:56), seeing Our Lord, rejoiced; and

John (cf. *Luke* 1:41), at the voice of Mary, the Mother of God, leapt for joy.

But if, when any appear to you, there is tumult and noise from without and earthly shows and threatening of death and all that I have spoken of, then know that the visitation is from the wicked.

Let this likewise be a sign to you: when the soul continues in terror, the presence is of the enemy. For the demons do not take away men's fear, as the great archangel Gabriel did for Mary and for Zachary (cf. *Luke* 1:13, 30) and he who appeared to the women in the tomb; but rather, when they see them afraid, they increase their phantoms, the more to terrify them, that then they may come on them and mock them saying, *Fall down and adore us*. (Cf. *Matt.* 4:9). The Greeks they did thus deceive, for among them they were thus taken for false gods. But Our Lord has not left us to be deceived by the devil, since when he made such appearances to Him, He rebuked him saying, *Get behind me, Satan; for it is written, The Lord thy God shalt thou adore, and him only shalt thou serve*. (Cf. *Matt* 4:10). Therefore, let the evil one be more and more despised by us. For what Our Lord said, He said for our sake, that the devils, hearing the same words from us, may be put to flight through the Lord, who in these words rebuked them.

We must not boast for having cast out devils, nor be proud for healings; nor must we admire only him who casts out devils and make naught of him who does not. But let a man study the strict living of each, and either copy and match it, or else better it. For to work signs is not ours. That is the Saviour's doing. So He said to the disciples, *Rejoice not because the devils are subject to you, but because your names are written in Heaven.* (Cf. *Luke* 10:20). For our names written in Heaven are a witness to our virtue and our life, but to cast out devils is simply a favor of the Saviour who gave it. Wherefore to those who boast of their miracles and not of their virtues, saying, *Lord, have we not cast out devils in thy name and wrought many miracles in thy name?* (Cf. *Matt.* 7:22), He answered, *Amen, I say to you, I know you not.* For the Lord knows not the ways of the unholy. (Cf. *Ps.* 1:6).

As I have said, it is absolutely necessary to pray to receive the grace of discerning spirits, that as it is written, we may not trust every spirit. (Cf. *1 John* 4:1).

I would now cease, saying nothing of my own, and being content with thus much only. But that you may not think these things are only my talk, but may be sure that I speak from experience and fact, for this reason, though I become as one unwise, yet the Lord who hears knows that my conscience is clean, and that not for myself but for your love and your profit do I repeat what I have seen of the practices of the demons. How often have they called me blessed, and I have cursed them in the name of the Lord. How often have they foretold about the water of the river, and I have said to them, "And what concern is that of yours?" Once they came threatening, and surrounded me with battle array, like soldiers. Sometimes they filled the house with horses and beasts and serpents, and I sang the psalm, *These in chariots, and these in horses, but we shall be magnified in the name of the Lord our God* (cf. *Ps.* 19:8), and at these prayers they were turned back by the Lord. Once in the dark they came with a show of light, saying, "We have come to light you, Antony." But I shut my eyes and prayed, and at once their unholy light was quenched. And a few months later, they came as if singing psalms and quoting the Scriptures, *and I as one deaf heard not.* (*Ps.* 37:14). Once they shook the monastery, but I prayed and remained unshaken in mind. And afterwards they came again, stamping, hissing and leaping. But as I prayed and reclined, singing psalms to myself, they at once began to wail and weep as if utterly exhausted, and I glorified God, who took away and made mockery of their daring and their fury.

Once a demon appeared to me, exceeding lofty, with phantom array, and dared to say, "I am the power of God, and I am His providence; what wilt thou that I bestow on thee?" Then I blew a breath at him, naming the name of Christ and endeavored to strike him; and it seemed to me that I had struck him, and instantly, vast as he was, he disappeared with all his demons at the name of Christ. Once when I was fasting, the deceiver came to me as a monk carrying phantom loaves, and gave me counsel, saying, "Eat, and cease from your many hardships; you also are a man, and you will lose your strength." I, knowing his craft, arose to pray, and he could not bear it, for he vanished, looking like smoke as he went out through the door. How often in the desert did he show me a vision of gold, that I might but touch it and look at it; and I sang a psalm against him, and it melted away. Often they struck me blows, and I said, *Nothing shall part me from the love of Christ* (cf. *Rom.* 8:35), and on that they struck each other instead. It was not I who stopped them and brought them to naught, but it was the Lord, who says: *I saw Satan like lightning falling from heaven.* (*Luke* 10:18). My children, I have transferred these things to myself, mindful of the Apostle's saying (*1 Cor.* 4:6), in order that you may learn not to faint in your hard life and not to fear the phantoms of the devil and his demons.

Chapter 10

THAT WE NEED NOT FEAR SATAN

Seeing that I have begun to discourse thus unwisely, take for your safety and encouragement this also. And believe me, for I do not lie. Once someone knocked at my door in the monastery, and going out I saw a tall and mighty figure. Then on my asking, "Who are you?" he said, "I am Satan." I asked, "Why are you here?" and he said, "Why do the monks and all other Christians blame me for no cause? Why do they curse me every hour?" When I said, "Then why do you annoy them?" he answered, "It is not I that annoy them, but they disturb themselves, for I am become powerless. Have they not read that *the swords of the enemy have failed to the end, and their cities thou hast destroyed? (Ps. 9:7).* I have now no place, no weapon, no city. Everywhere are Christians, and now the desert too is grown full of monks. Let them watch themselves, and not curse me without cause." Then I, marveling at the grace of the Lord, said to him, "Liar though you always are and never speaking truth, yet this time you have spoken true, even against your will, for Christ has come and made you powerless and cast

you down and disarmed you." He, hearing the
Saviour's name and not enduring the burning heat
thereof, disappeared.

Now if the devil himself confesses that he can
do nothing, we ought utterly to condemn both
him and his demons.

The enemy, then, with his hounds has all these
wicked arts, but we who have learned his weakness are able to despise them. Therefore, let us
not droop in mind in regard of this, nor ponder
terrors in our soul, nor weave affrights for ourselves, saying, "But how if a demon come and
overthrow me, or lift me and hurl me down, or
appear suddenly and craze me with fear?" Such
things must not enter our minds at all, nor must
we be sad as though perishing. Rather we must
be brave and glad, as men who are being saved.
Let us bear in mind that with us is the Lord, who
defeated them and brought them to naught. And
let us always believe and ponder this, that, while
Our Lord is with us, our enemies shall not touch
us. For when they come, as they find us, so do
they themselves become to us: they fit their phantoms to the mind they find in us. If they find us
in fear and panic, at once they assail us, like
thieves who find the place unguarded; and all that
we of ourselves are thinking, that they do and
more. For if they see us afraid and cowardly, they
increase our fear yet more by phantoms and
threats, and thereafter the wretched soul is
punished in these ways. But if they find us glad

in the Lord and pondering on the good things to come and thinking thoughts of God and accounting that all is in God's hand and that a demon avails naught against a Christian nor has power over any—seeing the soul safeguarded with such thoughts, they turn away in shame. So the enemy, seeing Job thus fenced about (*Job* 1:21), fled from him; but finding Judas bare of these thoughts (*John* 13:2), mastered him. Therefore, if we would despise the enemy, our thoughts must always be of God and our souls always glad with hope, and we shall see the toys of the demons as smoke and themselves fleeing instead of pursuing, for they are, as I said, very cowardly, always expecting the fire that is prepared for them.

This sign also keep by you to cut off fear of them: When any vision comes, do not begin by falling into panic, but whatever it be, first ask bravely, "Who are you, and whence?" and if it be a vision of the good, they will satisfy you and change your fear into joy. But if it is anything diabolical, at once it loses all strength, seeing your spirit strong; for simply to ask, "Who are you, and whence?" is a proof of calmness. So when the son of Nave questioned (*Jos.* 5:13) he learned, and the enemy was discovered when Daniel (*Dan.* 13:54, 58) questioned him.

—Book III—

ANTONY'S WORK FOR OTHERS

Chapter 11

THE PERSECUTION
UNDER MAXIMINUS

As Antony made this discourse, all rejoiced. It increased the love of virtue in some, in some it cast out carelessness, and in others it ended self-conceit. All were persuaded to despise the plottings of the devil, admiring the grace which God had given to Antony for the discerning of spirits.

The monasteries in the hills were like tents filled with heavenly choirs, singing, studying, fasting, praying, rejoicing for the hope of the life to come, laboring in order to give alms, having love and harmony among themselves. And in truth it was like a land of religion and justice to see, a land apart. For neither wronger nor wronged was there; nor plaint of tax-gathering; but a multitude of ascetics, all with one purpose to virtue; so that, looking back on the monasteries and on so fair an array of monks, one cried aloud saying: *How lovely are thy dwellings, O Jacob, thy tents, O Israel; like shady groves, and like a garden by a river, and like tents that the Lord hath pitched, and like cedars beside the waters.* (*Num.* 24:5-6).

Antony himself retired as usual to his own monastery by himself and went on with his holy life, groaning daily at thought of the mansions of Heaven, longing for them and seeing the shortness of man's life. For when going to food and sleep and the other needs of the body, shame came on him, thinking of the spirituality of the soul. Often when he was to eat with many other monks, the thought of the spirit's food came back on him, and he excused himself and went a long way from them, thinking it shame that he should be seen eating by others. Yet he ate alone, for the needs of the body; and often too with the brethren, ashamed on their account, but emboldened by the words of help he gave them. He used to say that we should give all our time to the soul, rather than to the body. A little time indeed we must of necessity allow to the body, but in the main we must devote ourselves to the soul and seek its profit, that it may not be dragged down by the pleasures of the body, but rather that the body be made subject to the soul, this being what the Saviour spoke of: *Be not solicitous for your life what you shall eat, nor for your body what you shall put on. (Luke 12:22). And seek not what you may eat or what you may drink, and be not lifted up; for all these things do the nations of the world seek. But your Father knoweth that you have need of all these things. But seek ye first his kingdom, and all these things shall be added to you. (Cf. Luke 12:29-31).*

After this, the persecution which then befell

under Maximinus overtook the Church. When the holy martyrs were taken to Alexandria, Antony also quitted his monastery and followed, saying, "Let us too go that we may suffer if we are called, or else may look on the sufferers." He had a longing to be martyred, but not wishing to give himself up, he ministered to the confessors in the mines and in the prisons. In the hall of judgment he was full of zeal for those who were called, stirring them to generosity in their struggles, and in their martyrdom receiving them and escorting them to the end. Then the judge, seeing the fearlessness of Antony and his companions and their zeal in this work, gave orders that none of the monks should appear in the judgment hall, nor stay in the city at all. All the others thought best to be hidden that day, but Antony cared so much for it that he washed his tunic all the more, and on the next day stood on a high place in front and showed himself plainly to the prefect. While all wondered at this, and the prefect saw as he went through with his escort, Antony himself stood fearless, showing the eagerness that belongs to us Christians; for he was praying that he too might be martyred, as I have said. He himself mourned because he was not martyred, but God was keeping him to help us and others, that to many he might be a teacher of the strict life that he had himself learned from the Scriptures. For simply at seeing his behavior many were eager to become followers of his way of life. Again, therefore, he ministered as before to the confessors, and as though sharing their bonds, he wearied himself in serving them.

When later the persecution ceased, and the Bishop, Peter of blessed memory, had died a martyr, Antony departed and went back to his monastery and abode there, a daily martyr to conscience, fighting the fights of the faith. He practiced a high and more intense asceticism; he fasted constantly; his clothing was hair within and skin without, and this he kept till his death. He never bathed his body in water for cleanliness, nor even washed his feet, nor would he consent to put them in water at all without necessity. Neither was he ever seen undressed, nor till he died and was buried did any ever see the body of Antony uncovered.

Chapter 12

IN THE HEART OF THE DESERT
(At Der Mar Antonios, Between the
Nile and the Red Sea)

When he retired and purposed to pass a season
neither going forth himself nor admitting any, a
certain captain of soldiers, Martinianus, came and
disturbed him, for he had a daughter beset by a
demon. As he stayed long, beating the door and
asking him to come and pray to God for the child,
Antony would not open, but leaned down from
above and said, "Man, why do you cry to me?
I am a man like yourself. But if you trust in Christ
whom I serve, go, and as you trust, so pray to
God, and it shall be done." And he at once believing and calling on Christ, went away with his
daughter made clean from the demon. Many other
things did the Lord through Antony, for He says,
Ask and it shall be given to you. (Luke 11:9).
For though he opened not the door, very many
sufferers simply slept outside the monastery, and
trusted and prayed sincerely and were cleansed.

As he saw that many thronged to him and that
he was not suffered to retire in his own way as
he wished, being anxious lest from what the Lord

did through him, either he himself should be lifted
up (cf. *2 Cor.* 12:6), or another should think
about him above the truth, he looked around him
and set out to go to the upper Thebaid, where
he was not known. He had got loaves from the
brethren and was sitting by the banks of the river
watching if a boat should pass, that he might
embark and go up with them. While he was thus
minded, a voice came to him from above: "Antony,
where are you going, and why?" He was not
alarmed, being used to be often thus called; but
listened and answered, "Since the crowds will not
let me be alone, therefore I want to go to the
upper Thebaid because of the many annoyances
here, and especially because they ask me things
beyond my power." And the voice said to him,
"Though you should go up to the Thebaid, or,
as you are considering, down to the pastures, you
will have greater and twice as great burden to
bear. But if you wish to be really alone, go up
now to the inner desert." Antony said, "And who
will show me the way, for I know it not?" And
at once he was shown some Saracens setting out
that way. Advancing and drawing near, Antony
asked to go with them into the desert, and they
welcomed him as though by the command of
Providence. He traveled with them three days and
three nights and came to a very high hill. There
was water under the hill, perfectly clear, sweet and
very cold; beyond was flat land, and a few wild
date-palms.

Antony, as though moved by God, fell in love with the place, for this was the place indicated by the voice that spoke to him at the river bank. At the beginning he got bread from his fellow-travelers and abode alone on the hill, none other being with him, for he kept the place from then on as one who has found again his own home. The Saracens themselves, who had seen Antony's earnestness, used to travel by that way on purpose and were glad to bring him bread; he had besides a small and frugal refreshment from the date-palms. Afterwards, when the brethren learned the place, they were careful to send to him, as children mindful of their father. But Antony, seeing that by occasion of the bread some were footsore and endured fatigue, and wishing to spare the monks in this matter also, took counsel with himself and asked some of those who visited him to bring him a pronged hoe, an axe, and some corn. When they were brought, he went over the ground about the hill, and finding a very small patch that was suitable, he tilled it and sowed it, having water in abundance from the spring. This he did every year, and had bread thence; being glad that he should trouble no one on this account, but in all things kept himself from being a burden. But later, seeing that people were coming to him again, he grew a few vegetables also, that the visitor might have some little refreshment after the weariness of that hard road. At first the beasts in the desert used to often damage his crops and his garden when they came for water, but he, catching one of the beasts, said graciously to all, "Why do you harm me when I do not harm you? Begone, and in the name of the Lord do not come near these things again." And thereafter, as though fearing his command, they did not approach the place.

He then was alone in the inner hills, devoting himself to prayer and spiritual exercise. But the brethren who ministered to him asked that they might bring him each month olives and pulse and oil, for he was now an old man.

How many wrestlings he endured while he dwelt there we have learned from those who visited him: not against flesh and blood (*Eph.* 6:12), as it is written, but against opposing demons. For there also they heard tumults and many voices and clashing as of weapons, and at night they saw the hill full of wild beasts, and him they saw fighting as with visible foes and praying against them. His visitors he comforted, but he himself fought, bending his knees and entreating the Lord. And it was indeed a thing to admire, that being alone in such a wilderness, he was neither dismayed by the attacks of devils, nor with so many four-footed and creeping things there, did he fear their savageness, but according to the Scripture (*Ps.* 124:1), he trusted the Lord truly like Mount Sion, with a mind tranquil and untossed; so that rather the devils fled, and the wild beasts kept peace with him, as it is written.

Thus the devil watched Antony and gnashed his

teeth against him, as David says in the psalm (*Ps.* 111:10), while Antony had consolations from the Saviour and abode unharmed by his wickedness and his many arts. He set wild beasts on him when watching at night. Almost all the hyenas in that desert, coming out from their dens, surrounded him. He was in their midst, and each with open mouth threatened to bite him. But knowing the enemy's craft, he said to them all, "If you have received power over me, I am ready to be eaten by you, but if you are sent by devils, delay not, but go, for I am Christ's servant." On this they fled, his words chasing them like a whip.

A few days after, while he was working (for he was careful to work), someone stood at the door and pulled the string of his work, for he was weaving baskets, which he gave to his visitors in exchange for what they brought. He rose and saw a beast resembling a man as far as the thighs, but with legs and feet like a donkey. Antony simply crossed himself and said, "I am Christ's servant; if you are sent against me, here I am," and the monster with its demons fled so fast that for very speed it fell and died. And the death of the beast was the demons' fall, for they were hasting to do everything to drive him back from the desert, and they could not.

Chapter 13

THE TEACHER OF MONKS

Once, being asked by the monks to return to them and oversee them and their dwellings from time to time, he set out with the monks who had come to meet him. A camel carried bread and water for them, for all that desert is waterless and there is no drinkable water at all except in the one hill where they had drawn, where his monastery is. On the way, the water failed, and they were all like to be in danger, the heat being extreme. For having searched around and found no water, they were now unable even to walk, but lay down on the ground and let the camel go, giving themselves up. And the old man, seeing all in danger, was very grieved, and groaning, went a little way from them and prayed, bending his knees and lifting his hands. And at once the Lord made a spring come forth there where he was praying, and so all drank and were refreshed. Filling their water-skins, they sought the camel and found it, for it happened that the rope had wrapped round a stone and so was held fast; they brought it back and watered it, and putting the skins on it, finished their journey unharmed.

When he came to the outer monasteries, all welcomed him, seeing in him a father. And he, as though he had brought with him supplies from the mount, entertained them with discourse and imparted help. So there was joy anew in the hills, eagerness to advance, and each drew courage from the faith of the rest. He too rejoiced to see the zeal of the monks and to find that his sister had grown old in her virginity and was herself a guide to other virgins.

After some days he returned to his hill. From that time many came to him, and some who were sufferers dared the journey. For all monks who came to him he always had this advice: to trust in the Lord, and love Him, to keep themselves from bad thoughts and bodily pleasures, and not to be led astray by the feasting of the stomach, (as it is written in Proverbs), to flee vainglory, to pray always, to sing psalms before sleeping and after, to repeat by heart the commandments of the Scriptures and to remember the deeds of the Saints, that by their example the soul may train itself under the guidance of the Commandments. Especially did he advise them to give continual heed to the Apostle's word: *Let not the sun go down upon your wrath*, and to consider that this was spoken about all the Commandments alike, so that the sun should not go down, not simply on our anger, but on any other sin of ours, for that it is right and necessary that the sun condemn us not for any sin by day, nor the moon for any fall or even thought by night. "To safe-guard this it is well to hear and observe the Apos-tle, for he says: *Judge yourselves and prove yourselves. (2 Cor. 13:5).* Daily then let each take account with himself of the day's and the night's doings, and if he has sinned let him cease; and if he has not, let him not boast, but abide in the good and not grow careless, nor judge his neighbor, nor justify himself, as the blessed Apos-tle Paul said, till the Lord come who searcheth hidden things. For often we miss seeing what we do, and we do not know, but the Lord misses nothing. To Him therefore let us leave judgment; with each other let us have sympathy and bear one another's burdens; ourselves let us judge, and where we fail be earnest to amend. For a safe-guard against sinning, use this manner of observ-ing: let us each note and write down our deeds and the movements of the soul, as if to tell them to each other, and be sure that from utter shame of being known, we shall cease from sinning and even from thinking over anything bad. For who likes to be seen when he is sinning, or having sinned, does not rather lie, wishing to hide it? Just as we should do no foulness in sight of each other, so if we write our thoughts as if telling them to each other, we shall better guard our-selves from foul thoughts, for shame of being known. Let the written tale be to us instead of the eyes of our fellow monks, that, shamed as much at writing as at being seen, we may not even think evil, and molding ourselves in this way, we shall be able to master the body, to please God and to trample on the snares of the enemy."

Chapter 14

MIRACLES

This was his instruction to those who visited him: To sufferers he gave compassion and prayed with them, and often the Lord heard him in many ways. He neither boasted when he was heard, nor murmured when not, but always gave thanks to God and urged the sufferers to be patient and to know that healing belonged not to him nor to any man, but to God who doeth when He will and to whom He will. The sufferers took the old man's words in place of healing, since they had learned to suffer with patience and not with shrinking, and the cured learned not to thank Antony, but God alone.

A man named Fronton from Palatium had a terrible disease, for he was biting his tongue, and his eyes were in danger. He came to the hill and begged Antony to pray for him. When he had prayed, he said to Fronton, "Depart and you shall be healed." Fronton objected and for days stayed in the house, while Antony continued saying, "You cannot be healed while you stay here. Go, and when you reach Egypt, you shall see the sign that is wrought on you." The man believed and went, and as soon as he came in sight of Egypt, he was freed from his sickness and made well, according to the word of Antony, which he had learned from the Saviour in prayer.

A girl from Busiris in Tripoli had a dreadful and distressing sickness, a discharge from eyes, nose and ears, which turned to worms when it fell to the ground; and her body was paralyzed and her eyes unnatural. Her parents, hearing of monks who were going to Antony, and having faith in the Lord who healed the woman troubled with an issue of blood (*Matt.* 9:20), asked to accompany them with their daughter, and they consented. The parents and their child remained below the hill with Paphnutius, the confessor and monk. The others went up, but when they wished to tell about the girl, Antony interrupted them and described the child's sufferings and how they had traveled with them. On their asking that these also might come to him, he would not allow it, but said, "Go, and you will find her cured if she is not dead. For this is not my work, that she should come to a wretched man like me, but healing is the Saviour's, who doeth His mercy in all places to them that call on Him. To this child also the Lord hath granted her prayer, and His love has made known to me that He will heal her sickness while she is there." So the marvel came to pass, and going out they found the parents rejoicing and the girl in sound health.

Two of the brethren were traveling to him when

the water failed, and one died and the other was dying; he had no longer strength to go [on], and lay on the ground awaiting death. But Antony, sitting on the hill, called two monks who happened to be there and urged them, saying, "Take a jar of water and run down the road towards Egypt, for two were coming, and one has just died, and the other will if you do not hasten. This has just been shown me in prayer." The monks therefore went and found the one lying a corpse and buried him; the other they revived with water and brought him to the old man, for the distance was a day's journey. If anyone asks why he did not speak before the other died, he asks amiss in so speaking. For the sentence of death was not from Antony, but from God, who so decreed about the one and revealed concerning the other. In Antony this only is wonderful, that while he sat on the hill and watched in heart, the Lord revealed to him things afar.

For another time also, as he was sitting there and looking up, he saw in the air someone borne along, and great rejoicing in all that met him. Wondering at such a choir and thinking of their blessedness, he prayed to learn what this might be. And at once a voice came to him that this was the soul of the monk Amun in Nitria. He had lived as an ascetic till old age. Now the distance from Nitria to the hill where Antony was is thirteen days' journey. Those who were with Antony, seeing the old man in admiration, asked to know and heard from him that Amun had just died. He was well known because he often visited there and because through him also many miracles had come to pass, of which this is one. Once, when he had need to cross the river called the Lycus, the waters being in flood, he asked his companion Theodore to keep far from him that they might not see each other naked in swimming the river. Theodore went, but he was again ashamed to see himself naked. While, therefore, he was ashamed and pondering, he was suddenly carried to the other side. Theodore, himself a devout man, came up, and seeing that Amun was first and unwetted by the water, asked to know how he had crossed. And seeing that he did not wish to speak, he seized his feet, declaring that he would not let him go till he had heard. Amun, seeing Theodore's obstinacy, especially from his speech, asked him in turn not to tell anyone till his death, and then told him that he had been carried across and set down on the other side, that he had not walked on the water, and that this was a thing not possible to men, but only to the Lord and those to whom He granted it, as He did to the great Apostle Peter. (*Matt.* 14:29). And Theodore told this after Amun's death.

Now the monks to whom Antony spoke of Amun's death noted the day, and when, thirty days later, the brethren came from Nitria, they inquired and found that Amun had fallen asleep at the day and hour when the old man saw his soul carried up. And both these and the others were all amazed how pure was the soul of Antony, that he should learn at once what happened thirteen days away and should see the soul in its flight.

Again, Archclaus the Count once met him in the outer hills and asked him only to pray for Polycratia, the renowned and Christ-like virgin of Laodicea, for she was suffering much in her stomach and side, through her great mortifications, and was weak throughout her body. Antony therefore prayed, and the Count made a note of the day when the prayer was made, and departing to Laodicea, found the virgin well. Asking when and on what day she was freed from her sickness, he brought out the paper on which he had written the time of the prayer; and when he heard, he immediately showed the writing on the paper, and all recognized with wonder that the Lord had freed her from her pains at the moment when Antony was praying and invoking the goodness of the Saviour on her behalf.

Often he spoke days beforehand of those who were coming to him, and sometimes a month before, and of the cause for which they came. For some came simply to see him, some through sickness, some suffering from devils. And all thought the toil of the journey no trouble or loss, for each returned feeling helped. Antony, while he said and saw such things, begged that none should admire

him in this regard, but rather should admire the
Lord, who grants to us men to know Him in our
own measure.

Another time, when he had gone down to the
outer monasteries and was asked to enter a ship
and pray with the monks, he alone perceived a
horrible, pungent smell. The crew said that there
was fish and pickled meat in the boat and that
the smell was from them, but he said it was different; and even as he spoke, came a sudden shriek
from a young man having a devil, who had come
on board earlier and was hiding in the vessel.
Being charged in the name of our Lord Jesus
Christ, the devil went out, and the man was made
whole, and all knew that the foul smell was from
the evil spirit.

Another came to him, one of the nobles, having
a devil. This demon was so dreadful that the possessed man did not know he was going to Antony;
also he used to eat the filth of his own body.
Those who brought him begged Antony to pray
for him, and Antony, pitying the youth, prayed
and watched the whole night with him. Towards
dawn, the youth suddenly sprang on Antony,
pushing him. His friends were indignant, but
Antony said, "Do not be angry with the youth;
it is not he, but the demon in him, for being
rebuked and commanded to depart into waterless
places, he became furious and has done this.
Therefore, glorify God, for his attacking me in
this way is a sign to you of the demon's going."

And when Antony had said this, the youth was at once made whole and then, in his right mind, recognized where he was and embraced the old man, thanking God.

Chapter 15

VISIONS

Many other such things are related by numbers of monks to have been done through him, and their stories agree. Yet these are not so marvelous as the greater wonders that he saw. Once when he was about to eat and stood up to pray, about the ninth hour, he felt himself carried away in spirit; and, a thing strange, as he stood, he saw himself as though out of himself and being guided by others through the air, also foul and terrible beings stationed in the air and seeking to hinder his passage. As his guides resisted, the others demanded a reckoning, if he were not liable to them. But when they would have taken an account from his birth, Antony's guides stopped them, saying, "All from the time of his birth the Lord has wiped out, but from the time he became a monk and promised himself to God, you can take account." Then, as they accused him but proved nothing, the path became free and unhindered for him, and he saw himself approaching and re-entering himself, and so once more he was Antony. Then, forgetting to eat, he remained the rest of the day and all the night groaning and praying.

For he was in amazement to see how many we fight against and with what great labors we have to pass through the air, and he remembered that this is what the Apostle said: *According to the ruler of the power of the air.* (Cf. *Eph.* 2:2). For herein has the enemy his power, in fighting and trying to stop those who pass through. For which cause he specially exhorted us: *Take ye up the armor of God that ye may be able to withstand in the evil day* (*Eph.* 6:13), *that having no ill to say about us* (*Titus* 2:8), the enemy may be put to shame. And let us who have learned this remember the Apostle's words: *Whether in the body I know not, or out of the body, I know not; God knoweth.* (2 *Cor.* 12:2). But Paul was rapt to the third heaven and heard words unspeakable, and returned; whereas Antony saw himself entering the air and struggling till he was proved free.

Another favor he had from God. When he sat alone in the mountain, if ever he looked into any matter with himself and could not see his way, it was revealed to him by Providence in prayer. He was one of the blessed who are taught of God (*John* 6:45), as it is written. So later, when he had had a discussion with some visitors about the life of the soul and the kind of place it will have hereafter, in the following night one called him from above, saying, "Antony, rise and go out and look." He went out (for he knew which voices to obey) and looking up saw a great figure, formless and terrible, standing and reaching to the clouds, and people going up as if on wings. And the figure was stretching out his hands, and some he stopped, and others flew above and, passing by him, rose without trouble thereafter. At these he gnashed his teeth, but exulted over those who fell. Then a voice came to Antony, "Understand the vision." And his mind being opened, he understood that it was the passing of souls and that the great figure standing was the enemy who hates the faithful. Those who are in his power he seizes and stops them from passing, but those who have not yielded to him he cannot seize, but they pass him by. Having seen this, he took it as a reminder, and strove the more to advance forward each day.

He did not willingly relate these things to others. But when he had long prayed and admired them in his own heart and his companions questioned and pressed him, he was forced to speak, being unable, as a father, to hide these things from his children, thinking also that while his own conscience was clear, the telling might be a help to them, teaching that the religious life bears good fruit and that often there is comfort for its hardships in its visions.

—Book IV—

ANTONY'S LAST YEARS

Chapter 16

HIS DEVOTION TO GOD'S CHURCH

Antony was by disposition long suffering and humble of soul. Being what he was, he yet reverenced the law of the Church exceedingly, and he would have every cleric honored above himself. He was not ashamed to bow his head before bishops and priests, and if ever a deacon came to him to seek help, he spoke what was needed to help him, but in regard to prayers he gave place to him, thinking it no shame that he too should be taught. For often he would ask questions and beg to hear his companions and acknowledge that he was helped if one said something useful. His face had a grace in it great and beyond belief. And he had this further gift from the Saviour: if he was with a company of monks and someone wished to see him who did not know him before, as soon as he arrived, he would pass over the others and run straight to Antony as if drawn by his eyes. Not by appearance or figure was he different from others, but by his ordered character and the purity of his soul. For his soul being at peace, he had his outer senses also untroubled, so that from the joy of the soul his face also was joyous, and from the body's movements one saw and knew the state of his soul, according to the Scripture: *When the heart is merry, the face is glad; when in grief, the face is gloomy. (Prov.* 15:13). So Jacob knew that Laban was devising a plot and said to his wives: *Your father's countenance is not as yesterday and the day before. (Gen.* 31:5). So Samuel knew David, for he had eyes that moved joy and teeth white as milk (cf. *1 Kgs.* 16:12). And so too was Antony known, for he was never troubled, his soul being tranquil; he was never gloomy, his mind being glad.

To the Faith his devotion was wonderful. He never held communion with the Meletian schismatics, knowing their wickedness and rebellion from the beginning, nor had friendly converse with the Manichees, nor any other heretics, save only to warn them to return to their duty, believing and teaching that their friendship and society was a harm and ruin to the soul. So also he loathed the Arian heresy and taught all neither to go near them nor partake in their ill-faith. Once when some of the Ariomanites came to him and he questioned them and found them misbelievers, he drove them from the hill, saying that their words were worse than the poison of serpents.

Again when the Arians lied about him, that he believed as they, he was grieved and angry with them. Then, urged by the bishops and all the other brethren, he came down from the hill, and entering Alexandria, denounced the Arians, saying this was the last heresy and the forerunner of Antichrist. And he taught the people that the Son of God is not a creature, neither is He begotten out of nothingness, but that He is the eternal Word and Wisdom of the Father's being. "Therefore, it is impious to say there was a time when He was not; for the Word was always co-existing with the Father. Wherefore, do ye have no fellowship at all with these most impious Arians, *for there is no fellowship of light with darkness.* (Cf. 2 Cor. 6:14). For you are devout Christians, but these who say that the Son and Wisdom of God the Father is a creature differ nothing from Gentiles, worshipping the creature before God the Creator. Be ye sure that the whole creation is aroused against these men, because they count among creatures the Creator and Lord of all, in whom all things were made."

The people all rejoiced to hear so great a man anathematize the heresy which attacks Christ. And all the citizens ran together to see Antony. Greeks, too, and even their so-called priests came to the church, saying, "We ask to see the man of God"— for so all called him. For there also the Lord through him cleansed many from demons and healed the mad. Many Greeks asked only to touch the old man, believing they should be helped. Naturally, in those few days as many became Christians as else one would have seen in a year. Some thought that he was annoyed by the crowds, and therefore were keeping the people from him, but he, untroubled, answered, "These are no more numerous than the demons with whom we wrestle in the hills."

When he was leaving* and we were setting him on his way, a woman from behind shouted, "Wait, man of God, my daughter is grievously troubled with a devil; wait, I beseech, lest I hurt myself running." The old man hearing and being asked by us, waited willingly. When the woman drew near, the child was hurled to the ground. Antony prayed and spoke the name of Christ, and the child rose up healed, the unclean spirit being gone out of her. The mother blessed God, and all gave thanks. And he too rejoiced, departing to the hill as to his own home.

---

* Socrates, *Hist.* IV, c. 25, relates an incident of this journey: It is said that earlier Antony had met this Didymus in the time of Valens, when he went down to Alexandria from the desert because of the Arians, and that finding the intelligence of the man he said to him, "Let not the loss of your bodily eyes trouble you, Didymus; for the eyes that are failing you are only such as flies and gnats also can see with. But rejoice that you have the eyes wherewith angels see, by which God is seen, and His light is received."

Chapter 17

THE GIFT OF UNDERSTANDING

He was extremely prudent. The wonderful thing was that, not having learned letters, he was yet a quick-witted and clever man. Once two Greek philosophers came to him, thinking that they could experiment on Antony. He was then in the outer hills. But understanding the men from their looks, he went out to them and said through an interpreter, "Why, O philosophers, have you toiled all this way to a foolish man?" And when they answered that he was not foolish, but very wise, he said to them, "If you have come to a fool, your labor is useless; but if you think me wise, then become as I, for we ought to imitate what is good. If I had gone to you, I would have imitated you; as you have come to me, become as I, for I am a Christian." They departed in wonder, for they saw that even demons feared Antony.

Some others of the same kind met him again in the outer hills and thought to mock him because he had not learned letters. Antony said to them, "And what say you, which is first, the mind or letters? And which is the cause of which, the mind of letters, or letters of the mind?" When they answered that the mind is first and is the inventor of letters, Antony said, "Then to one whose mind is sound, letters are needless." This answer astounded both them and the listeners. They went away marveling to see such wisdom in a plain man.* For he had not the rough character of one who is reared in the hills and grows old there, but he was both gracious and courteous. His speech was seasoned with the wisdom of God, so that none had ill-will against him, but rather, all rejoiced on his account who went to see him.

Later, some others came. They were of those who among the Greeks seem to be wise. When they asked from him an account of our faith in Christ and tried to argue about the preaching of the Cross of God and wished to scoff, Antony waited for a little, and first pitying them for their ignorance, said through an interpreter (who could render his words excellently), "Which is nobler: to confess the Cross, or to attribute adulteries and impurities to those who among you are called gods? For to say what we say is a sign of manly courage, a proof of contempt of death, but yours is a yielding to lewdness. Next, which is better: to say that the Word of God was not changed, but

---

* One of the philosophers came to the holy Antony and said, "Father, how do you keep up without the comfort of books?" And Antony said, "My book is nature, and whenever I will, I can read the words of God." (Socrates, *Hist.* IV, c. 23.).

remaining the same, took to him a human body to save and help men, in order that, sharing our human birth, he might make men sharers of the divine and spiritual nature, or to liken the divine to senseless things, and for that cause to worship beasts and serpents and images of men? For these are the things worshipped by you who are wise. And how do you dare to scoff at our saying that Christ has appeared as man, when you make the soul come from Heaven, saying that it had strayed and fell from the vault of Heaven into the body?—and would that it were only into the body of man, and not shared with beasts and serpents. Our faith declares the coming of Christ to save men, but you talk amiss of the soul unbegotten. We believe the power of Providence and His love of men, that this also is not impossible with God; but you, calling the soul an image of the spirit, impute falls to it and make fables of how it can be changed. And now through the soul you are making the spirit too a thing changeable. For as was the image, so needs must be that of which it is the image. And when you thus deem about the spirit, bear in mind that you are blaspheming also the Father of the Spirit.

"And touching the Cross, which would you say is better: when plotted against by wicked men to endure the Cross and not shrink from any manner of death whatever, or to tell tales of the wanderings of Osiris and Isis, and the plots of Typhon, and the flight of Kronos, and swallowings of children and slaying of fathers? For this among you is wisdom. And if you mock at the Cross, why do you not marvel at the Resurrection? For those who tell of the one wrote the other, too. Or why, when you remember the Cross, do you say nothing of the dead who were raised, the blind who saw, the paralytics who were cured and the lepers made clean, the walking on the sea and the other signs and wonders which show Christ, not as man, but as God? To me it seems that you are utterly unfair to yourselves and that you have not honestly read our Scriptures. But do you read them and see that the things which Christ did prove Him to be God dwelling with us for men's salvation.

"But do you also tell us your own teachings. Though what could you say about brute things except brutishness and savagery? But if, as I hear, you wish to say that these things are spoken among you in figure, and you make the rape of Persephone an allegory of the earth and Hephaestus, lameness of the fire, and Hera of the air, and Apollo of the sun, and Artemis of the moon, and Poseidon of the sea; nonetheless, you are again worshipping that which is no god; you are serving the creature instead of the God who created all. For if you have made up these tales because of the loveliness of the world, you are right to go as far as admiring it, but not to make gods of creatures, lest you give to things made, the honor of the Maker. In that case, it is time you should hand over the architect's honor to the house he has built, or the general's honor to the soldier. Now, what do you say to all this?—that we may see if the Cross has anything that deserves to be scoffed at."

As they were quite at a loss, turning this way and that, Antony smiled and said again through the interpreter, "All this is clear even at first sight. But since you lean rather on proofs and arguments and because you have this art, you want us also not to worship God without reasoned proofs. Do you first tell me this: How comes sure knowing of things, and especially knowledge about God? Is it through reasoned proof, or through a faith which acts; and which is the earlier, the faith that acts, or proof by reasoning?" And when they answered that the faith that acts comes earlier, and that this is the sure knowledge, Antony said, "You say well, for that faith comes from the very build of the soul, but the art of logic from the skill of those who framed it. It follows that, to those who have an active belief, reasoned proofs are needless and probably useless. For what we know by faith, that you are trying to establish by argument. And often you cannot even put in words what we know, so that the action of faith is better and surer than your sophist's proofs.

"Now, we Christians hold not our secret in the wisdom of Greek reasonings, but in the power of a faith which is added to us by God through Christ Jesus. For proof that this is a true account, look how without learning letters we believe in

God, knowing from His works, His providence over all things. And for our faith being a force which acts, look how we lean on the belief in Christ; whereas you lean on sophistical debates, and yet your monstrous idols are coming to naught, while our faith is spreading everywhere. And you with your syllogisms and sophisms do not draw any from Christianity to Hellenism; we, teaching faith in Christ, despoil your superstition, for all are learning that Christ is God and the Son of God. You with all your beauty of speech do not stop the teaching of Christ, but we by naming Christ crucified drive away all the demons whom you fear as gods. And where the Sign of the Cross comes, magic fails and poisons do not work.

"For tell me, where are now your oracles, where the incantations of the Egyptians, where the phantoms of magicians? When did all these cease and fail, but at the coming of the Cross of Christ? And is it the Cross then that deserves scorn, and not rather the things which by it have been made void and proved powerless? For this is another wonderful thing, that your teaching was never persecuted, but was honored by cities publicly, while the Christians are persecuted, and yet it is we and not you that flourish and grow. Your teachings, praised on all sides, guarded on all sides, perish; while the faith and teaching of Christ, mocked by you and persecuted by kings, has filled the world. For when did the knowledge of God so shine out? When did chastity and the virtue of virginity so show itself, or when was death so scorned as since the Cross of Christ came? And this none doubts who looks at the martyrs scorning death for Christ's sake, or looks at the virgins of the Church, who for Christ's sake keep their bodies pure and undefiled.

"These are sufficient proofs to show that for serving God, faith in Christ is the only true faith. Even now, behold, you who seek conclusions from reasonings, you have no faith. But we do not prove, as our teacher said, in persuasive words of Greek wisdom; we win men by faith, which lays hold of real things before argument can logically establish them (cf. *1 Cor.* 2:4). See, there are some standing here suffering from demons (they were people who had come to him beset by demons, and bringing them into the midst he said): Either do you make them clean by your syllogisms and by any art or magic you wish, calling on your idols, or if you cannot, then cease attacking us, and see the power of the Cross of Christ." Having said this, he invoked Christ, and signed the sufferers with the Sign of the Cross twice and thrice. And at once the men stood up, whole now and in their right mind and blessing God. And the so-called philosophers were astonished and really stupefied at his wisdom and at the miracle that was done. But Antony said, "Why do you wonder over this? It is not we that do it, but Christ, who does these things through those who believe in Him. Believe, then, you also; and you will see that what we have is not tricks of words, but belief through a love that is active unto Christ, which if you also have, you will no longer seek proofs by reasonings, but will think faith in Christ sufficient by itself."

This was Antony's discourse. The men wondered at it and departed embracing him and acknowledging that they had been helped.

Chapter 18

THE ARIAN PERSECUTION

The renown of Antony reached even to kings. For on hearing of these things, Constantine Augustus and his sons, Constantius Augustus and Constans Augustus, wrote to him as to a father and begged to receive answers from him. He, however, did not value these writings nor rejoice over the letters, but was just what he had been before the kings wrote to him. When the letters were brought to him, he called the monks and said, "Do not admire if a king writes to us, for he is a man, but admire rather that God has written the law for men, and has spoken to us by His own Son." He wished not to receive the letters, saying that he knew not what to answer to such. But being urged by the monks because the kings were Christians and they might be scandalized as though he made them outcasts, he allowed them to be read. And he wrote back, welcoming them because they worshiped Christ, and advised them, for their salvation, not to think much of things present, but rather to remember the coming judgment, and to know that the only true and eternal king is Christ. He begged them also to be lovers of men, to care for justice and to care for the poor. And they were glad to get his letter. So was he beloved by all, and so did all wish to hold him as a father.

With this character, and thus answering those who sought him, he returned again to the mount in the interior and continued his usual life. Often when sitting or walking with visitors he would become dumb, as it is written in Daniel. (Cf. *Dan.* 10:15). After a time he would resume his former discourse with the brethren, but they perceived that he was seeing some vision. For often in the mountain he saw things happening in Egypt, and described them to the Bishop Serapion, who was within and saw Antony occupied with the vision. Once as he sat working, he became as in ecstasy, and in the vision he groaned constantly. Then after a time he turned to his companions groaning; and trembling, he prayed, bending his knees and abiding a long time; and when he arose, the old man was weeping. Then the others trembled and were much afraid and begged him to tell, and long they urged him till he was compelled to speak. Then with a great groan he said, "Ah, my children, better is it to die than that there happen what I have seen in this vision." And when they asked again, he said with tears, "Wrath shall overtake the Church, and she shall be delivered up to men who are like to senseless beasts. For I saw the table of the Lord, and around it mules standing on all sides in a ring and kicking what was within, as might be the kicking of beasts in a wild frolic. You heard surely," he said, "how I was groaning, for I heard a voice saying, 'My altar shall be made an abomination.'"

So the old man said, and two years after came this present onset of the Arians and the plundering of the churches, wherein, seizing by force the vessels, they had them carried away by pagans; when, too, they forced the pagans from the workshops to their meetings and in their presence did what they would on the sacred table. Then we all understood that the kicking of the mules had foreshown to Antony what the Arians are now doing, brutishly as beasts. When he saw this vision, he comforted his companions, saying, "Do not lose heart, children, for as the Lord has been angry, so later will He bring healing. And the Church shall quickly regain her own beauty and shine as before. And you shall see the persecuted restored and impiety retiring to its own hiding places and the True Faith in all places speaking openly with all freedom. Only, defile not yourselves with the Arians. For this teaching is not of the Apostles, but of the demons and their father the devil; and indeed from no source, from no sense, from a mind not right it comes, like the senselessness of mules."

Chapter 19

HIS SPIRITUAL INFLUENCE

Such was the life of Antony. We must not disbelieve when all these wonders are wrought through a man. For it is the promise of the Saviour, who said: *If you have faith as a grain of mustard seed, you shall say to this mountain, Depart hence, and it shall depart; and nothing shall be impossible to you.* (*Matt.* 17:19). And again: *Amen, amen I say to you, if you ask the Father anything in my name he will give it to you. Ask and you shall receive.* (*John* 16:23, 24). And it is He who said to His disciples and to all that believe in Him: *Heal the sick; cast out devils; freely you have received, freely give.* (*Matt.* 10:8).

Antony healed, therefore, not as one commanding, but praying and using the name of Christ, so that it was plain to all that the doer was not he, but the Lord, who through Antony showed His tenderness for men and healed the sufferers. Only the prayer was Antony's, and the ascetic life for the sake of which he had settled on the mountain, glad in the contemplation of heavenly things, grieved that so many disturbed him and dragged him down to the outer hills. For the judges all wanted him to come down from the mount, since it was impossible for them to go there because of the pleaders who followed them. But they asked him to go that they might only see him. He disliked and declined the journey to them. But they would hold their ground and send the prisoners up to him with soldiers, that by reason of these, he might perhaps come down. So being constrained and seeing them lamenting, he used to go to the outer hills, and his toil was not wasted, for to many he was a help and his coming a benefit. He helped the judges, counseling them to value justice above all else and to fear God and to know that with what judgment they judge, with such shall they be judged. (*Matt.* 7:2). Yet he loved his abode in the hills above all other.

Once when he was thus constrained by those in need, and the officer of the soldiers had begged him by many messengers to come down, he went and discoursed a little on matters of salvation and on their own needs, and then was hastening back. On the captain asking him to stay longer, he answered that he could not be long with them and satisfied him by a beautiful comparison, saying, "As fish that are long on dry land die, so monks who linger among you and spend much time with you grow lax. Therefore, we have to hasten to the hills as the fish to the sea, lest if we linger, we should forget the inner life." The officer who heard this and much more from him said in admiration that surely this was a servant of God, for whence came wisdom so high and so great to a mere man, unless he were beloved of God?

There was one officer, named Balakios, who sharply persecuted us Christians in his zeal for the abominable Arians. Since he was so cruel as to beat virgins and strip and flog monks, Antony sent to him and wrote a letter to this intent: "I see wrath approaching you; cease, therefore, persecuting Christians, lest the wrath overtake you, for even now it is nigh upon you." Balakios, laughing, threw the letter on the ground and spat on it, and insulting the bearers, told them to take this message back to Antony: "Since you are anxious about the monks, I will now pay you a visit also." And five days had not passed when the wrath overtook him. For Balakios and Nestorius, the prefect of Egypt, went out to the halting place of Chaireos, the first from Alexandria; and they were both riding on horses. These belonged to Balakios, the quietest he had. But before they reached the place, they began to play with each other, as horses do, and suddenly the quieter of the two, on which was Nestorius, biting Balakios, threw him down and fell upon him, and so tore his thigh with its teeth that he was carried back to the city at once and died in three days. And all men marveled how what Antony had foretold was quickly fulfilled.

In such wise did he warn the cruel. But others who came to him he brought to such a mind that they forgot straightway their disputes at law and esteemed those blessed who withdraw from the world. But if any were wronged, he so defended them that one would think that he himself, and not other persons, had been wronged. He had such influence for good over all, that many who were soldiers and many of the wealthy laid aside the burdens of their life and became monks. He was, in fact, like a healer given to Egypt by God. For who went to him in sorrow and did not return in joy? Who came mourning for his dead and did not quickly put aside his grief? Who came in anger and was not changed to kindness? Who sought him desperate in his poverty, and hearing him and seeing him, did not learn to despise wealth and take comfort from poverty? What monk grown careless but became stronger from visiting him? What youth ever came to the mount and looked on Antony but soon renounced pleasure and loved self-denial? Who came to him tempted by devils and was not freed? Who came with troublous thoughts and gained not peace of mind?

For this was another great thing in Antony's holiness, that having, as I have said, the grace of discerning spirits, he knew their movements and was not ignorant to what object each of them leans and impels. And not only was he himself not befooled by them, but others who were beset in their thoughts he taught how they might defeat their snares, explaining the weakness and the wickedness of the tempters. Each, therefore, as

100 ST. ANTONY OF THE DESERT

though anointed by him for the fight, went down emboldened against all the contrivings of the devil and his demons.

Again, how many maidens who had suitors, seeing Antony only from afar, remained virgins for Christ? From foreign lands, too, men came to him, and having received help with the rest, returned as if sent forth by their father. And since he died, all are like fatherless orphans, comforting each other with the bare memory of him, and cherishing his teachings and his counsels.

Chapter 20

HIS DEATH

The manner of the end of his life I ought also to tell, and you to hear eagerly, for this also is a pattern to imitate. He was visiting as usual the monks in the outer hills, and learning of his end from Providence, he spoke to the brethren saying, "This is the last visiting of you that I shall make, and I wonder if we shall see each other again in this life. It is time now for me to be dissolved, for I am near a hundred and five years." Hearing this, they wept, clasping and embracing the old man. But he talked joyously, as one leaving a foreign town to go to his own, and bade them "not to fail in their labors nor lose heart in their strict life, but live as dying daily; and, as I have said before, to be earnest to guard the heart from unclean thoughts; to vie with the holy; not to go near the Meletian schismatics, for you know their wicked and profane heresy; nor to have any fellowship with the Arians, for the impiety of these is plain to all. Be not troubled if you see judges protecting them, for their triumph will end; it is mortal and short-lived. Therefore, do ye keep yourselves clean from these and guard the tradition of the Fathers, and above all the loving faith in our Lord Jesus Christ, which you have learned from the Scriptures and have often been put in mind of by me."

When the brethren pressed him to stay with them and die there, he would not for many reasons, as he implied without saying, but on this account chiefly: To the bodies of religious men, especially of the holy martyrs, the Egyptians like to give funeral honors and wrap them in fine linens, but not to bury them in the earth, but to place them on couches and keep them at home with them, thinking by this to honor the departed. Antony often asked the bishops to tell the people about this, and likewise shamed laymen and reproved women, saying it was not right nor even reverent, for that the bodies of the patriarchs and prophets are preserved even till now in tombs, and the very body of Our Lord was put in a sepulchre and a stone set against it hid it till He rose the third day. He said this to show that he does wrong who after death does not bury the bodies of the dead, holy though they be. For what is greater or holier than the Lord's body? Many, therefore, hearing him, buried thenceforward in the ground and thanked God that they had the right teaching.

Now knowing this, and fearing lest they might so treat his body also, Antony hastened and took leave of the monks in the outer hills, and returning to the inner hills where he was used to dwell, he fell sick after a few months. He called those who were there (they were two who lived in the house, who had been fifteen years in the religious life, and ministered to him because of his great age) and said to them: "I am going the way of my fathers, as the Scripture says (cf. *Josue* 23:14), for I see myself called by the Lord. Be you wary and undo not your long service of God, but be earnest to keep your strong purpose, as though you were but now beginning. You know the demons who plot against you, you know how savage they are and how powerless; therefore, fear them not. Let Christ be as the breath you breathe; in Him put your trust. Live as dying daily, heeding yourselves and remembering the counsels you have heard from me. And let there be no communion between you and the schismatics, nor the heretical Arians. For you know how I also have avoided them for their false and anti-Christian heresy. So do you also be earnest always to be in union first with the Lord and then with the Saints, that after death, they also may receive you into everlasting tabernacles as known friends. Ponder these things, and mean them. And if you have any care for me, and remember me as your father, do not allow anyone to take my body to Egypt, lest they should deposit it in houses, for that is the reason why I entered the mountains and came here. And you know how I have always reproached those who do this and bade them stop the practice. Therefore, care for my body yourselves and bury it in the earth, and let my words be so observed by

you that no one shall know the place but yourselves only. For in the Resurrection of the dead
I shall receive it back from the Saviour incorruptible. Distribute my garments; the one sheepskin
give to Athanasius the bishop, and the cloak I used
to lie on, which he gave me new, but it has worn
out with me; and the other sheepskin give to Serapion the bishop, and do you have the hair-cloth
garment. And now God save you, children, for
Antony departs and is with you no more."

Having said this and been embraced by them,
he drew up his feet; then gazing as it seemed on
friends who came for him, and filled by them with
joy, for his countenance glowed as he lay, he died
and was taken to his fathers. Then they, as he
had given them orders, cared for his body and
wrapped it up and buried it there in the earth,
and no man yet knows where it is laid save only
those two. And they who received the sheepskins
of the blessed Antony and the cloak that he wore
out, each guard them as some great treasure. For
to look on them is like looking on Antony, and
to wear them is like joyfully taking on us his
teachings.

This is the end of Antony's life in the body, as
that was the beginning of his religious life. And
if this is but little to tell of such virtue as his,
yet from this little do you judge what manner of
man was Antony, the man of God, who from
youth to such great age held unchanged his keen
quest of a better life, who never for old age

yielded to the desire of varied meats, nor for failing strength of body changed his form of dress nor even bathed his feet with water. And yet in all respects he was to the end untouched by decay. He saw well, his eyes being sound and undimmed; and of his teeth he had not lost one, only they were worn near the gums, through the old man's great age. In feet and hands, too, he was quite healthy, and altogether he seemed brighter and more active than all those who use rich diet and baths and many clothes.

That he was everywhere spoken of and by all admired and sought even by those who had not seen him—these things are proof of his virtue and of a soul dear to God. For Antony was known not for his writings, nor for worldly wisdom, nor for any art, but simply for his service of God. That this is God's gift none could deny. For how was he heard of even to Spain and to Gaul, to Rome and to Africa, he sitting hidden in the hills, unless it were God who everywhere makes known His own people, who also had in the beginning announced this to Antony? For though they themselves act in secret and wish to be unnoticed, yet the Lord shows them as lanterns to all, that even from this the hearers may know that the Commandments are able to be fulfilled, and so may take courage on the path of virtue.

Now, therefore, read this to the other brethren, that they may learn what should be the life of monks and may believe that our Lord and Saviour

Jesus Christ glorifies them that glorify Him, and not only brings to the kingdom of Heaven those who serve Him to the end, but even here (though they hide themselves and seek retirement) He makes them everywhere known and spoken of for their own goodness and for the helping of others. And if need arise, read it also to the pagans, that perhaps thus they may learn not only that Our Lord Jesus Christ is God and the Son of God, but also that through Him the Christians, who serve Him sincerely and who piously trust in Him, not only prove that the demons whom the Greeks think gods are no gods, but trample on them and drive them out as deceivers and corrupters of men, through Christ Jesus our Lord, to whom is glory for ages of ages. Amen.